LOVE'S
FLORELOQUENCE

LOVE'S
FLORELOQUENCE

WENDY ANN WEBB

To the human condition – LOVE
and its opposite: Indifference
Two sides of one coin: Love/Hate; Indifference/Inconsequence

To my better half and our children
(in the stars and on earth)

INHERIT THE EARTH
MODERN CLASSICS

LOVE'S FLORELOQUENCE

By

WENDY ANN WEBB.

OTHER BOOKS BY THE AUTHOR
2022 Landscapes, David Norris-Kay & Wendy Webb/CT
Meek/Amazon.co.uk
2021 Persephone Weakens, Selected Poems 1996-2020/Volumes 1 & 2
(WWB)
2019 Whose Name was Wit in Waterr (WWB, Autobiography)
2016 Bevin Boy (WWB, Father's Biography)
2010 A Mermaid's Tale and Other Poems (WWB)
2008 Salvador Dali Paints Juliet (Indigo Dreams, 1st Prize
Winner/Ronnie Goodyer)
2006 Coasting Norfolk (Poetry Monthly Press/Martin Holroyd)
2000 Paradise Mislaid and Found (Partners/Ian Deal)
1998 In Step With a Carpenter (QQ Press/Alan Carter)
1998 Rocky Start. Diary of a Special Care Baby (WWB/Bliss,
Biographical)
2001 Tips (Issues 1-94), 2013-2020 Star Tips (Issue 140)

LOVE'S FLORELOQUENCE

By

WENDY ANN WEBB

PUBLISHER: Inherit The Earth Online Publishing
ISBN: 9798372967595

CONTENTS

5

2004 BLUSHING VEILCHENBLAU MEETS SEXY REXY
Tips 2006-09/PUBLD

'My love is like a red, red rambling rose'
made vigorous by pruning every year
so darling romance blossoms sky's trousseaux,
paints ripe blush summer autumn-rich not sere.
Dusk's Fragrant Cloud plays Handel's palest mink:
bold sweetbrier stirs in twilight's atmosphere,
plucks sprays of Wedding Day cream, tinted pink.
Exquisite slate: damp's charming crazy-pave;
'An English Beauty' romps and rolls, flush minx.
Blush, Lovely Lady, pulsing sweetmeat navel.
Blue Rambler love will open lush-gold thatch,
hands train each prick to lintel's architrave;
inviting inglenook - dough's fresh-baked batch.
Fuelled Aga hearth. Rise, Sexy Rexy's match.

2011 FORGETTING LOVE
2017-12/PUBLD Star Tips 122

I wonder if she doesn't like remembering?
Preferring peace of absence to forget.
And will I ever know, or be considering
this question down the line, and with regret?

I wonder if it's too painful, or too tetchy
to scrooge the ghosts of Christmas past, grown strong?
Or whether it's more personal – this gets petty –
to understand the many things gone wrong.

I wonder if this mirror's steamed? A fairground
silent image, screaming game, distorted
warp-wrapped reality of love; so proud
of all that's been achieved. Aged skin contorted

and yet love's love when alteration's found,
with champagne, flowers and comfort proving sound.

2006 FOLDING NAPKINS ON LOVE
[Insp by *Tiffany Atkinson, Aberystwyth]. Tips/2008-01

'A person is the space they spare for those they love'*
in endless cups of coffee, tea,
in kitchens floured for the family meal
and in the poured aperitif of talk.
They lay a knife, a fork, a spoon
and soon spill words as thick as gravy sauce.

No space is barer than an absent chair,
for that is where the person goes,
whose invitation has expired, to eat
and satiate the space with loving food.

Is it too rude to ask whose seat is bare
as salt spilled into linen's crease,
where love deceases cellars bare of wine.
It's fine to condiment a meal
and yet unfeeling spacelessness is left
to wash and rinse and dry when guests have gone.

2008/008 ALL YOU NEED
Dawntreader/Issue 18/2012-03/PUBLD

Hands fumble across calculator,
as numerals make no sense
and don't add up. All you need.
Stumbling into the red, all digits blur.
Need, need, all you need,
this aching bank vault of my heart
that loves and loves and always
all you need is like an empty balance
endlessly revolving my brain's track:
love is all you need's stuck groove.

2005 UNPEELING CHURCH BELLS
PRELUDE When Botticelli Met Goldilocks/2007/PMP

On life's unmounted tarmac where she drove
- revs welcoming for others' families -
she prayed. God heard. With eyes berthed on the road
she laughed, then saddled groomsman; promised child.

Soon after, she was coasting Norfolk reeds
to family transplanted – late – from Greece.
Learnt laughter's gentle love-worn, surgeon's skill:
sawn heartbeats stitching through their ribcage home.

While newly grilled and friendless, she soon cruised
to local Norwich church and 'Solo' grey;
her heart enlarged late hope, she feared decline,
till barbecued aromas singed a mate.

Her crook lock soon secured a pair of eyes:
enticing as hands hooked round steering wheel.
With legs spread, circling clutch, she – green - espied
a mounting, gentle smile, revved welcoming.

Then navigation notched a shocking gear,
(red hair's sauced BBQ endeared dull slate).
Wild autumn charmed, to route his broken heart.
'Map reading's soonest mended to new dreams.'

Night rider fantasy sailed muse-wet broads;
good tread - his dignity - recovered slow.
He dallied with a boat; house; travel bug
and, in the Rockies, melded his cold heart.

A fresh volcano (from Canadian flights)
touched down - at Norwich - passion's magma heat.
Her lava flow was ashen by delays;
it drove eruption's plug – as stars – sky high.

A Robin miracle soon sheathed (bride-white).
Hood's horn peeled marble - plenty charmed as psalms.
No Michelangelo drove manhood's rise…
sweet infant David. Wherry berthed on cue.

10

1998 DRESSED FOR THE OCCASION
Linkway/2001-11; A Bard Hair Day/Partners

Love to love may prove
a laundry for soiled garments,
rinsed and spun and dried -
till colours fade, thread-weaves bind.
Neither claims odd socks or bra.

Prove me not, my love,
your weave is coarse, my weft fine,
dress us not in rags.
Cut out patterns, bright and plain,
a complement for cocktails.

1997 CRACKING ACORNS
Paradise Mislaid and Found/1999-09/Partners

Your wounded pride hides, as a drooping flag,
whose pole surrenders in its Autumn damp.
Hard pavements crack profuse, their acorn brag,
and shrivelled sparrow leaves drift Winter's stamp.
Your manhood's rousing chorus puts to flight
dark hordes of soldier sea ants in your skies,
migrating to a private Oscar night,
yet senseless that deft cuts deny their prize.
In sympathy, you're "rousing chorus" sore,
life's walking wounded cut off in its prime.
Performance cauterised at manhood's core,
you limp offstage, raw tinder quenched, this time.
Your op. was just a snip at nature's drain,
before Spring's tendrils reap a deeper pain.

11

2002 SWIMMINGLY, DEAR TROUT
Linkway/2001-08; Nursing Creature of the Deep/2001/WWB

Earth has not anything to show more fair
than you, sleek trout, my lover, lying near.
Your flesh so pink and warm, so succulent
with gleaming butter sauce pooled on my plate.
A slice of lemon squeezed tart on your skin,
firm almonds crunched between my teeth, so fine.
Such scratch of bones are smoothed and tossed aside,
consumed by Midas' touch of golden seeds.
Yet there's the rub, in nature's finest hour,
too faint, worn brass, your dish has lost its power.

1999 A LOVE POEM
Paradise Mislaid and Found/2000/Partners

You were there in birth and death,
in sex and mess,
in dirth and mirth
and roses blooming with apology.

You were there beginnings, ends,
you made amends.
You smiled your pin-prick stars in blackest night
and lightened with your touch.

Is it too much to mouth the words
of love, of lust, of longings lost?
       And found.

2004 HE ROSE TO AUTUMN'S PYRE
[Insp by Edmund Waller and Algernon Charles Swinburne] Tips/2006-07

You, lovely, rose
in timely joy to sweet desire
and, in ache's throes,
you satiated my dark pyre
and quenched your smoke to dust, to seed my words with fire.

2000 SHIPS IN THE NIGHT
Reach/2000-06/PUBLD; Rocky Start/2000/WWB

Bewitch me with the honey of your breath
        so sickly sweet,
devour me with the pinprick of your need,
in sensuous mess.
Thrum drumbeats in my ears with seashell surf
and Braille-dot love upon our shifting sands.

Press kisses on a simple rosebud mouth
        no scent, no breeze,
stretch fingerprints of dainty little hands
still stained with ink.
Blush wonder in those clustered cherry toes
then howl a love bereft and damned at sea.

Delight and hang on every frail new breath
and bleep and flash,
entwine our fingers in a plastic womb
so sticky, damp.
Stroke down-hair, trembling, fine between each wire
and laugh at nappies armpit length and free.
Stare long as words describe a foreign land
        then calm accept,
wipe twenty futile games of sweat and tears,
unsullied yet.
Tip-touch across an ocean with no shore
and flutter lips as ships pass in the night.

2001 THE OAK AND THE WILLOW CAT WENT TO SEA
Nursing Creature of the Deep/2001/WWB

Cradled slowly in your crotch, the breeze swells
thick with whispers, and tantalising leaves.
A blush of autumn curves into the knot
of intertwining branches, spiked with pain.
The oak and willow groan, rough bark and smooth,
as catkins tickle acorns, round and firm.

Is life so ridiculed, so fanciful –
a thrash of limbs raised hard against the sky?
Is dust so fine, it tickles ribs with clouds
and scuds white flesh, like surfers on the tide?
Shall Adam, banned from Eden, learn the art
of clothing Eve in Paradise once more?

The oak is done, his sap submerged at sea,
a willow tickles catkins on his shore.

2003 A LOVE-NEGATING LIFE
Writing Magazine Poetry Workshop/2003-09; Reach 2004-09

Never to feel the wonder of first love,
counting stars, wrapped in courting's firm embrace.
Never to give a self so he may prove
your soul mate more than all the human race.

Never to fight so that his worth excels,
to play a little cold so fires may burn.
Never to vow quicksilver's dross repels;
your love bands bud - each rose plucks his concern.

Never to drape around his friendly voice,
to banter on the phone like chores are dead.
Never to know this home is his first choice:
your parting only near as life's fine thread.

You could have sparked bright orbs, joined to your man.
You could have birthed his children's bubbling span.

2003 IF LOVE IS SWEETER
Metverse Muse, India/2011-03

If you can savour love as others fall foul,
and lose your heart, yet blame no female charm.
If you trust again, throw in no wimpish towel,
but let your family see you reach no harm.
If you echo-sound the depths of Windermere,
or climb Ben Nevis and return by dark,
or visit Eden, yet keep your love sincere,
tease thistles, leeks, not roses in the park.

If you taste each dish, claim not to be the cook,
yet super-star one mistress in your house.
If you warm to friend or foe through mirrored look,
to save shame's face, read culture in a mouse.
If you coo dull seconds, lightly as a dove,
with wit and stamina to match life's span.
Then earth is clover, wrapped in a mother's love,
and – what is more – you'll bless your woman's man!

2001 JUST A SPARKLING RED SKY AT NIGHT
Nursing Creature of the Deep/2001/WWB

A piece of string, no sparkle, no panache,
a cord to fit the hollow of a neck.
With little room to spare, I wondered why
my lover drew it quite so tight today?

My Valentine he had been, year on year
and bonds were drawn between his heart and mine.
One final noose might slacken or break free,
a tether could unleash a heart chained taut.
But Cupid's arrows slow-sparked bright each night
and slavishly beamed lighter every day.

His gift, a sparkle, carefully adorned,
a shepherd's sky delight blazed night on night.

2003 HAPPILY DEFROSTING PARADISE
Quantum Leap/Summer 2003; PERSEPHONE Vol 1/2021

Happiness is a sneaked kiss at the checkout,
a girlish holding of hands and queueing for ice cream,
a meal for two outrageously sublime
as others consider children, beer or sport.

Happiness is love on ice, on the edge,
a meeting for chilli and rice.
Strange how wedding bells and white soon gleam
confetti-bright with life in rainbow's prism.

Happiness, as a child, chases the butterfly,
poeticises each slice of life,
cares not a fig for bearing Euro fruit -
creates an Eden full of apple cores.

So strange that consummation's lesser known
than knowledge as an evil good, a loss of Paradise.

2004 MAN ON A SUMMER'S DAY
Norfolk Poets' Garden/2006/PMP

Shall I compare you to a watering can?
You get too hot as sun chances upon our lawn
and you're thirsty when those flowers blush or nod.
How willing, hothead, to – manly – fill your spout
and dribble just enough to make them bloom.
My, is your silver stubble, oh, so smooth
and how your shape reflects 'stages of man'.
You are modern just in sheen and yet inside
you're hollowed out and spent when you're not full.
Ah, man, such stainless steel, I love you still.

2004 LOVE STAGED IN A LAUNDRY
A Bard Hair Day/2004-10; Flying to Never Land/2005/PMP

Love does not age
nor sour fast
when consummation's wedded bliss
is bound in weekly cycle:
the toil of white and coloureds,
mixed with socks and woollens,
will fill and rinse and spin again
into the finest off-white of pure love.

Love does not age
nor sour fast
when raven locks gleam with new grey,
when sparkling eyes are dulled by drudge
and baggy jumpers bag no more.
Yet love is in the commonplace of hearts.

Sweet Juliet may whine like her fat nurse
and Romeo, long lost to aches and pains,
locks love – those balcony day – in memories of bliss
and more, much more in blissful loving ways.
Tucked into humdrum of a daily meal
and wine, a little, for the chill
and brochures brought home trophy-rich,
though never packaged for a hotel flight.
Shoes are cobbled; ironing's creased
into familiar loving stage
for actors playing ageless magic love.

Love does not age
nor sour fast
and grows forever old as earth is young.
Do not grieve - for poignancy - like death,
for love shines as the evening star
and man, at every stage, has come of age.
Poets darn no darling socks
- true loves buy socks from Asda.

17

2004 SLEEPING TOGETHER
Reach 2008-01 (Readers' Vote 3rd); PERSEPHONE Vol 1/2021WWB

I love you through the watches of the night
in warm caressing eddies: drowsing flesh,
toes wriggling, dip in shoreline's hazy breath,
where senses touch in simple second sight.

I love to feel the covers net our flight,
so sleep with me, think tangled words not less
than waking with me to a little death.
Your wreck an impotence of captured might.

Abandonment, dream's skin, a shifting dune,
composing shallow lullabies to love.
Bare fireflies light our dark, we need no moon.
Hands' softest adorations stroke, ungloved,
reflection's stars in waterless lagoon.
So shall your heart its true devotion prove.

2022 VALENTINE SHORTS
Web Star 2022-02

Love is like a red, red rose,
that only blooms in June.
In Feb it's cold and prickly and
as constant as the moon.

Will you be my Valentine?
I only want a cuppa:
no wine, nor chocs, nor meals (sublime),
though I'm tasty as a Pukka.

2004 BIRTHDAY BOY

Reach/2005-06; Celebration of Love/2006/PMP

Ah, hothead June, I know your birthday well,
when you can bake in summer's heat, or I
could bake a cake: commiserate on years
and stroke that hair, still rich, or balding pate,
awaiting night to show my pleasure still.
Joining you for the empty pint or two,
in bottoms up to barley, apple's bite…

Or we could not stay home, to hop and roam
in homely sunset of a village pub;
a meal for two, no roaring fire, just haze
of every summer past since we first met –
and how the setting sun would burnish love
to furnish trinkets – dust free – for next year.
But I will rage against offending drudge,

that keeps the grudge of precious time from you,
when duty rains, a freak storm to my beach
and driftwood roams the oceans to my shore.

I wish for more, for endless space to care
and match your cloudy socks and glimpsing sun -
peeking a toe to bathe in clear blue skies,
as bottles rise to shore; your messages

forever tender, calms against life's storm.
Stay with my warmth, my Aga to your pain.
Let heat caress and drain your tiredness, stress.
Romance me in the mess of everyday,
for all our travel brochures lie at home;
your Caribbean sunset floods through me.
So, birthday boy, where is that birthday suit?

2004 ATTRIBUTES OF LOVE (Ghazal, 'Eyre Broad', a name)
Metverse Muse/Muse 'Clad in Costumes'/ Summer 2010

Your cheeks are wide, your welcome long,
your eyes dance, green, your nose formed strong.

Your lips adhere, so warmly fat
beside the fire you're happiest at.

Your brows mock-shock, your welcome long,
your ears, though large, can do no wrong.

Your stubble chin, though rough and dark,
shaves smooth as milk: licked, sipped – a lark.

You hide your teeth - they fail to please -
which I will part, to please and tease.

Your raven hair, your nose formed strong;
your heady brow can do no wrong.

Your hands caress to love's intent,
enfolding arms so heaven-meant.

Your feet so large they fail to please,
your legs fine-rigged to please and tease.

Your bum's not neat, but it's still fine
and, best of all, it's mine, all mine.

Your lids as bags, they fail to please,
so rest and dream, don't wheeze and sneeze.

Your midlife gut, not prone to beer
but curry feasts we share, my dear.

Your frame is fine, to please and tease,
but poor frail chest don't wheeze and sneeze.

Your love, it's true, can do no wrong
while this heart keeps your welcome long.

Contd

20

Your tide will wash to beach-pure sand,
parched sailor – love – you drink my land.

Eyre's driftwood praise – Broad nose formed strong –
my vessel tides your welcome, long.

2005 A PERFECT FINISH
Norfolk Poets' Garden/2006/PMP

Let me be the whisper through your moistened lips,
let my vintage quench you, through enchanted sips.
Let your tongue slide slowly, savouring all drips,
let your heady feeling rose-scent fruiting hips.

Bloom to sweet perfection, finest perfect rose.
Set, fragile and tender, damp-paint pristine prose.
Overblown, fade softly, hips of fattened hose,
watered, fed and fertile; pruned stump – winter's close.

2004 * WEDDINGS AND * FUNERAL(S)
Anthology/Autumn 2005/Forward Press

* weddings and * funeral(s), it must be fifteen years,
and now my suit, although it's best, is mothballed full of fears.
I cannot open wardrobe door and wreathe its dust in sheets
without recalling trousers creased into such varied seats.

If I could live my life again, a new suit I would buy
so that my bedroom no more lived endangered by a sigh.
I would ensure a jolly cloth, to make me laugh out loud
and to each ceremony skip, less starched but much too proud.

The vicar's quip, 'You're much too late,' – or 'Wedding's booked next week,'
and I could grin from here to here, as Fred's most festive freak.
My granddaughter, most whitely miffed, by my recounted tale,
might pat me on my ageing pate, hiss ' That suit's now for sale!'

My walk, unaided by a stick, though serious gait might show
if I turned up with mournful stare for mother's Romeo.
The ex, now there's a thought, so fine, such sport could flow so free
if I chose right: annoying grief; or smile and whoop of glee.

* weddings and * funeral(s), I think I know the score,
it seems to me the voting's rigged, now I've passed sixty-four.
The sums grow more conservative, so when it's time to go,
I've slept through wakes till no-one's left - but vicar - for my show.

I've made a deal, I've now struck gold, there's one last special gig,
if I must wear my suit again, I'll dress it with a fig.
My birthday suit will suit me fine; don't dress me in a shroud.
I've spread the word to guarantee my launch attracts a crowd.

Meanwhile my suit's upon a Guy, that soon goes up in smoke,
I lost few pounds for charity, a stylish hippie joke.
* weddings and * funeral(s), my ratings can't go down;
hip jazz and jive, hop's beaming nude: the finest swinger in town.

2004 IN PRAISE OF LADY LUCY
[Wordsworth tribute] PERSEPHONE Vol 1/2021

Strange fits of passion I will tell
to all who read this ode,
sweet Lucy's star will never sell;
the black sky's her abode.

None cares a jot for my sweet girl,
eyes violet, moss and dull.
None praise her petals, they unfurl
like rocks, so fat and full.

So only death is kind to her;
no grave is less unknown.
I love her, though none others stir,
applause grows more full-blown.

I love her like a rose in June,
when dark disguises thorns.
My eyes moon nature's distant tune,
dilemma's dressed in horns.

Dream Lady Lucy rides me high
to passions fitting, strange.
The moon and Equus raise a sigh;
my planets rearrange.

Such wayward fancies slip and slide
into my loving head,
if mounted on my steed I glide
within my Lucy's bed.

2004 SHEEP, EVERY DAY
Poetic Hours/ Spring 2005

Sheep, every day,
sheep, like clouds scudding skywards.
Across the valley: sheep,
her sheep.
He counted them nightly in his dreams.
Sheepishly he penned a plan
to round them up with sheepdog skills,
as he whistled loud at bleating air
and slept the shepherd's sleep dip
of mangers at shearing time.

Carefully he laid the feed
in sheepish letters on his hill:
'I love you' spread his woollen yarn,
'be mine...' for cloven hooves to tread;
he tended sheep at feeding time.

Across the valley: scudding sheep,
her sheep flocked in, but his spread out
to feed on sheepish dreams – and crook
his ewe into a shepherd's arms
and count no sheep at night.

And though she read his woolly flock
of loving letters, penned by hooves,
poor Cupid had shot wide his mark –
her heart was counting cowherds at the farm.

Our woolly ram shall end this tale,
for Eros, with his quiver fat,
will find a feckle, fatted ewe
who soon will not be counting sheep.
All night her ram will shear her heart;
at lambing time she'll count – like you –
how full his quivered love must be,
if he can bleat 'Be mine' by day
and knit a woolly jumper every night.

24

2005 SHADOW DANCING, OR, A TRICK OF THE LIGHT
Celebration of Love/2006/PMP

I will awaken sleepy morning light
to you, my Valentine, since I will go
around my daily chores, a rose of right
cupped in my palms, bloom-ripe, to hold - just so -

to you, my Valentine, since I will go
sweet with your gift's consuming bite.
Cupped in my palms, bloom-ripe, to hold just so:
my hands, a vase in silhouette, a sleight,

sweet with your gift's consuming bite.
See shadows dancing close through curtains' show;
my hands a vase in silhouette, a sleight
of sight, of faces facing, kissing slow.

See shadows dancing close, through curtains' show,
around my daily chores a rose of right;
of sight, of faces facing, kissing slow.
I will awaken sleepy morning light.

2005 STAR STRUCK
Tips 45/2005-12; PRELUDE/2007

He was my friend the first day that we met
and set my heart on fire
and roused my flesh
to spark a future starred into the past.
But would it last to flow
so like a river's thrusting source.

A past recoursing future in a dream.
We met and then we grew.

25

2005 MOTHER'S DAY
Linkway/2006-02

Morning rises to cards
and mouth-watering chocolates;
he will consume the best first.
Later: flowers. Best pink, scented, for a girl.

Best night on the town,
although it's day;
best restaurant, best food, best show
and, oh, best company.

Meal, home or away,
to brush and suit his fancy:
simmering soup and bread and fizzing coke.
Never roast, always Sunday best.

Desserts at home:
crackling cinema confectionary.
Premiere screening,
finest seats and treats and nibbles,
always well-prepared.

Best tickets in the house,
priced and best-stamped.
Simply the best of girlie treats:
seated between extra-special boys,
the best in town.

Later - best of all -
curry and wine when they're in bed
and chocolates for dessert…
if they're not rustling empty.
Otherwise, the very best of dads
for mum's special day.

2005 RED WINE, SALT CURED
Rejections Pile/2007-10/WWB

Red wine spills on white linen,
quickly absorbed by salt staining.
Absenting scent of spray and surf
and seashell murmuring, tossing golden apples
to Aphrodite's tones of other tides.

Fluttering of fingertips on skin,
drumming hope into creases.
Crumpling clothes in folds of flesh,
enfolding future's bare demands.
Scrape of chair on floor;
tacky hands fumbling to adjourn.

Rigging dropped and stashed;
clambering below deck, to softest lighting,
tickling fancy on crumpled sheets.
Coarse hair rubs softer skin,
rocking gently as masthead clanks;
intimately drunk to love's spilt wine,
staining salt and spray.

2005 THE RIGHT KEY
Flying to Never Land/2005/PMP

I wonder
when you lift the lid,
run finely-tuned fingers over my ivories,
test a chord,
slip between whites and blacks,
whether you know the score.
Or sheet music plays you,
hammers to my strings,
as I sing melodies of love.
Does music choose musician?
My instrument.

2005 DROPPING BALLS
Flying to Never Land/2005/PMP

Her injury left susceptibility to pain,
like strain mending silently, unobserved.
Age leant no splint to bounce back.

Her twinges sang, Country and Western,
stilettos and Stetson, like her Caesar scar
on a cold day, his snip and tuck, snook and stuck.
Anonymous as middle-aged spread,
bouncing balls at Wimbledon.

Her anxiety spread like hot flushes
late period; a miscarriage of justice.
Steaming impotence as a bed bath
running hot and cold, thermostat knackered.

Her bounce had bounced:
40 – Love, sagged and bagged
by stretch marks, love handles
and a load of - bouncing - balls.

Her breakdown recovery truck
- H.R.T. – out of fashion
as death, and sex beyond a certain age.
Restraining raging hormones?
Recklessly engineered ball bearings:
Jazz, Beat, heat, defeat.
So neatly slip into a little number
- classical as chemise, French knickers,
suspenders.

Oh, the balls of it, oh, the Blues of it,
oh, to rhythm-rage against the dying light:
Dylan, raise your glass; drink, and bottoms up.

2005 LEAVE ME EVERY TIME
Tips Pamphlet/2005-06/PUBLD

Leave me every time
but come back soon,
for I believe in you
and you in me.

So leave me every time
you have to go.
Please believe I'm so relieved
when you come home.

Leave now, each moment,
dress me close to suit.
Wear me in your skin and please believe
I wish you speed and safety to my arms.

Leave me every time
clutched to your sleeve
and I believe our love, worn well,
undresses into rest.

Leave me moments, every time,
I wear the skin your love's lived in.
Never ever leave me,
leave me to grieve.

2017 T FOR TWO
Crystal/2022-05

I'm pouring out a cup's imagination
while changing, powdering my nose; and such...
to write to ten – commandments or green bottles –
so you'll infuse and nibble, lick off cream,
groaning, satisfied; a little sick
of my imperfect free verse rhyming poem.
And then, at 3pm, you'll sigh, relax,
breathe cold air, squint at glowering autumn sun:
taking your eyes off that image of afternoon,
as I place my tee, aim and swing
into the rough (or lake) yet again.

29

2005 MORNING GLORY
Quantum Leap/2006-11; Editor's Cut 10th Anniv/QL

I want to share my unlight with you,
to wake up slowly to your feeling.
You ache in darkness so close to me.
I want to share my unlight, my feeling.

I want to see the darkness of your face,
to feel the shielded curtain of your body.
To taste your densest shadows; cheek's tense cheek.
I want to see the darkness, your body.

I want to taste consuming passion's mouth,
to savour urgent darkness in wide smiling.
White light is dancing slowly, morning's rise.
I want to taste consuming passions, smiling.

I want to scent and sense your fervent entry,
to fly into the sky's bright morning glory;
to applaud, with thunder, your waterfall.
I want to scent and sense your morning glory.

I want to share my unlight with you,
to wake up slowly to your feeling.
You ache in darkness so close to me.
I want to share my unlight, my feeling.

2005 TUSCAN SUNSET
Tips Pamphlet/2006-04

Wine's empty glass:
my sea's skies drunken with love / your
wine's empty glass.
Full-bodied vine, fruity, top class,
mixing dry red; sweet white; blends more
like rosé's drunken sunset. Shore-
wine's empty glass.

2005 LANDSCAPE OF BREAD
Poetic Hours/2005-09; PERSEPHONE Vol 1/2021

You bake the focus in my background's scene,
the oven-rock that rises on flat plain;
smoke figure leading in, until I lean
a panoramic backdrop's tempting lane:
You are gentle on my eyes.

You are the friendly face within a crowd,
a long-lost childhood placescape in a day;
a music, rich as thunder, thrilling loud,
when all I do is hang on what you say.
You are gentle on my ears.

You are the scent of curry, beer or wine;
of sweat, or night-breath, or the richest urge
to stir in juice that savours your love, mine,
fermenting brew's aromas as they merge;
you are gentle scent and taste.

You are cool breeze upon my cheek or ear,
soft tickle of fine hair upon my neck;
the scratch of stubble heaving pump-hearts near;
shock-ache of Roman baths, to brook a beck.
You are gentle to my touch.

You are my meteor in a God-filled heaven;
a navigation light to sail past hell.
You dough my flesh into a sweeter leaven;
delicious scent or taste, where all is well.
You are gentlest on my flesh.

2005 SHROUDED LOVE

[Insp by 'Espanā, Aparta De Me Este' by Caliz César Vallejo, trans. Robert Bly]
Poetic Hours/2006-06

Our love of the night before was still damp,
holding faded petals of stained laundry,
for yesterday was a long time ago,
suds lost in the hum of the washing machine.
'But the corpse… went on dying.'

Our love of a hundred nights and mornings,
like sludge after a chilled and frosty fall;
though seasons budded to a brighter spring,
love's ache had vanished in the common touch.
But the corpse went on dying.

Our love, a thousand dark and stormy nights:
hay tossed to bales of sustenance in barns.
Doors slammed to warm long winter drifts ahead,
passing before the endless sights of guns.
But the corpse went on dying.

Our love, ten thousand strokes of fickle time,
grey flicker of dull TV screens where life
expired before curved query's feeble eyes,
where common love was death and no hope raised.
But the corpse went on dying.

Our love, a million brushes in God's hands,
where paint was blood and sweat and sorrow's tears
and death, uncomely bright as love deceased,
where eyes wrapped shrouded vacancy of touch
and the corpse slowly stood up.

2005 FLORAL TRIBUTES FOR MY VALENTINE

[Insp by Amateur Gardening, February 2005, 'Meaning of Flowers']
Norfolk Poets' Garden/2005-09

My sweet is like a red carnation
delivered, full of optimism.
Presenting an upright bunch, says
in floriography:
'my heart aches for you.'
I'll return a scented handkerchief
and narcissus, 'stay sweet as you are.'

Why did my love send yellow sweet briar?
Now my love-lies-bleeding.
Misreading my sweet bright petals
for yellow: 'egotism.'

I will not swoon, I'll return jonquils:
'love me and return my affection.'
He'll be mortified his prickly briar
read sadly: 'love in decline.'
Dare I wear sad forget-me-nots,
or – like the hero – will it sweep him away?
He must be mine, I will remember the vine,
send him ivy 'Poetica.'

His bunch arrived, but pointed down,
I fainted all that day,
till I read 'perfected loveliness'
was the message of white camellias.
That evening he sent azaleas,
wrapped around with honeysuckle.
I read him true, blushed white to pink;
his message: 'save yourself for me.'
He's climbed my bustle and crinoline form
with 'generous love and devotion.'

My mother, dear, said 'Candytuft'
was a suitably prim reply.
'Indifference,' indeed, from her maybe;
I sent the sweetest almond.

Contd

His retort? Rose, Lord Penzance:
his pert bunch played with me.
My bodice tight, my basque constricts,
could he think my 'love in decline?'
Giggling, the parlour maid loosened my ties
at my earlier 'stupidity.'

Symbology was full of thorns,
would our love flower to holding hands?
I stroked cyclamen, gazed wanly abroad in:
'resignation and goodbye.'

My love sent 'spirited' freesia,
pale lilies: 'pure and sweet.'
Decorated with 'baby's breath'
and iris: 'my compliments.'

My love is mine no longer,
for when I sent a rose: 'true love,'
the florist arranged it with mignonette:

'Your qualities surpass your charms.'

2000 HARD DRIVE
Reach/2000-05; Nursing Creature of the Deep/2001/WWB

You ran the download, timed out, late at night,
no cosy room for two in sofa tryst,
toyed late with skittish mouse to drive her home
and downed a beer or two then dialled again.
Your hard computer brain was satisfied.

At dawn your chorus rang a serenade
a love song more familiar, less in code,
your downtime, then and now, was all for me
until your body, sated too, could rest.

2005 PERSONAL REPLY
[Insp by Wanda Edwards' 'Personal Ad']. 2009/09/QL Editor's Cut,
10th Anniversary

Dear wobbly wiggly lady,
I hope I'm not too late.
Your vintage, chase-pressed vigour
out-mounts scales over-weight.

Please let me paw, with gladness,
your bouquet-scenting face;
hung loose with lacy knickers.
My, how my heart may race.

I'll scratch those wrinkly love-bars,
mount naughty 'wobbly chair'.
Squeeze ample wiggly bottom,
chew finger-fine white hair.

I whisper, sweet, gruff nothings:
chocolate drops will pert your pout.
Birds may nest, my teeth are yours;
cat tails will mews love out.

My prime bone's yours, please wag too:
Dear Lady, I'm your Tramp.
Post Box: Battersea Dogs' Home.
I'll beg. Please lick my stamp.

2005 SLEEP SOFTLY
Tips Pamphlet/2006-04

Breathe sleep's deep low,
the heart rests softly when it's still.
Breathe sleep's deep low,
the gilt of peace to gift and flow
while quenching depths in afterglow.
A chalice quest, where souls who know,
breathe sleep's deep low.

2005 'SO WE'LL KISS NO MORE AND TELL, DEAR'
['So, we'll go no more a roving' by Lord Byron] Wordsworth
Footsteps/2006/PMP

So we'll kiss no more and tell, dear,
though love aches and flames flash strong
and deep hearts thump ever nearer,
pounding hearth where we belong.

For although we breathe together,
sword to sheath's combusti-on,
our strapped scabbard hearts' whenever
fuels slit-sparking unison.

Though slashed lunar face wanes nearer
eclipsing night's gashed day,
yet we'll no more kiss and tell, dear,
homely love's cosmic replay.

1997 SEA EYES
Broadly Norfolk/1999-05/PUBLD

Wild arrows arch between your heart and mine
an arc of promise and a tender sign,
a blush becalms the sea-eyes next my cheek
and beckons heart-buoys as I hear you speak.
A crimson rose now seals our eager lips,
cool mind-games dance between our subtle quips;
deft hands dissolve the distance fathoms deep
and, decked with sea-legs, reef the hearts we keep.
Calm echoes reach our eddied verve in time,
each billowed breeze is stretched with thoughts sublime.
A fleet now sails beyond the harbour's reach,
a fleeter crew lifts storm jib, lest we beach.
We gaze beyond the mirage ocean drifts
and glean our own wild arrows, loving gifts.

2005 MADONNA OF THE FLOWER WELCOMES DAVID
Roundyhouse/2008-06; PERSEPHONE Vol 1/2021

Please rub my fancy, and again tonight,
to tighten to the throb of your desire,
a rising fleur-de-lys of burning fire.
I'll open wide the mind of rare delight,
fair David's innocent but marbled form
of peeling Campanile, firm and stout,
beside a Virgin domed into a pout.
Consume cool petals, pert before a storm.

All Florence aches to flower in such space:
flood's artful Chantress, Neptuned wild with damp,
where ruination's spent, a bloated tramp.
Then chanting Latin blood dulls into grace.
Bridge me to day, and days' last night to night;
my fancy's thrilled, full-blown in dazed delight.

2004 BLUES FOR MARY OF THE ROCKS
Reach/2005-01/PUBLD; CELEBRATION of Love

Betrothed with three rings, engaging tale of
something old, something new, something borrowed…
each blue as her eyes, deep as the ocean.
Librans celebrate birth, a New Year gift.

So virginal, the sapphire gleamed first love,
encircled by each sparkling diamond star.
This ring, withdrawn to take a band of gold,
enclosed a clutch of infants, each a prince.

A pregnant, gleaming topaz, ripe, brand new,
conjoined at finest points in twining gold.
Love's letters knotted, they would never part
and romance shone, a comet in its course.

A cache of borrowed vouchers, now well-used,
another topaz, firmly set and blue.
'Crossed lovers' garnished synchronicity
and accent jewels, as 'Mary of the Rocks'.

Romantic novels told engaging tales,
quaked loving assignation's cocktail match
to consummate, in prose, erotic blues.
Yet as the stars that never failed to shine

and as the oceans, deeper than first love,
and as New Year, a gift of constancy,
first ring, unasked, was washed and strayed its hand
and faithful love burned, bought another orb

which snapped after a season, well insured,
and so this Heathcliff rushed to Argos' moors,
a safer gem was slipped on Catherine's hand.
No Linley had a chance to steal his love.

Think of the gleaming stars, they were her eyes,
insurance, simply paper from the store.
Sea's breezy smile, her face, for three wise men,
her lover crossing sails on gems, not rocks.   *Contd*

38

But I will end as good rhymes always should,
leaving sensuous hints of consummate blues.
Assistant wisely asked, 'Will you insure?'
'You bet!' they laughed... sealed love with peck and pen.

2005 IVORY WEDDING ANNIVERSARY
PRELUDE/2007/PMP

D'you think how I sat next to you and ate
a solitary sausage from my plate?
Though it was burnt, the solo BBQ
was pricked and forked before the day was through.
My love, do you remember?

We entered the walled garden for a walk
and scented morish blooms from bouquet talk.
A heady brew, where brushing hands was silk,
and touch a giggling ass in bathing milk.
My love, do you remember?

Do you remember, you were on your knees,
your only aim wet kisses and to please.
You asked me twice, to twice walk up the aisle:
to Sign, to March, to Kiss and reconcile.
My love, do you remember?
The crook lock was a best man's cobbled speech,
the pond ice, frozen, knobbled to my reach.
Your sausage was consumed upon my plate,
so pricked with forked champagne and burnt till late.
My love, do you remember?

2006 VALENTINE'S DAY
Metverse Muse/Summer 2007

A dozen roses, red and true
where every little helps to bloom
two hearts to beat in time, not rue
more faded petals in the room.
Discard foul water, veined true blue
to vase a vibrant foetal womb
where sac's replenished every day
to source a new life into play.

A bottle cracked to flow bright red
with liquor poured to glasses, two,
where sparkle's ready with no dread
and joy is brimming up to you.
To sip, to savour, lick the thread
of dripping silk served in a shoe.
Taste champagne into blush-beat pace
where eyes gaze on a loving face.

A box of chocolates to share
where heads brush close in sensuous touch
and hands, though hesitant, compare
each sweet for scent-rich form, so much
that sticky morsels taste like prayer
where silence rises into such
a look that could be cut to shape
a heart with melted letters' drape.

2006 JOYOUS FLIGHT
[Insp by 'Eternity' William Blake] Rejections Pile/2007/WWB

He who bends himself to a joy
does no wingèd life destroy;
for he who kisses, joyous flies,
lives eternity's sunrise.

A breath of kisses on the breeze
flutters brightly laden trees.
Sound joy sings full light's birdsong praise,
breeds conjoined in lengthened days.

Deep scents of heady gardens bloom,
soon Midsummer's drifts assume,
while harmonies raise fertile airs,
feathered synchronising pairs.

Young lovers bridal train each kiss,
aisles of joyous sunset-bliss.
Age gazes on eternal skies,
kisses dark at light's sunrise.

2006 ABSENCE MAKES THE GLASS...
Rhymin Romeo (1st Prize) 2006; SALVADOR/2008/IDP

Your glass half empty, for it's sipped for one
away from home and in a foreign town.
You bottoms-up and leave and swipe the key
of your hotel room where your work's half-read.
You stay up late, for there's no-one to share
an early night, to warm the sheets and flesh
until sleep wraps, exhausted, into one
where dreams are knotted to a rising dawn.
My glass half full, the bottle's still too rich
for solitary company to pour
in unaccompanied TV, to view
life lived in vital unions of stress.
No matter, you will text or phone night's brief,
adoring moments breathed till love's release.

2006 MAKE LOVE NOT WAR
[In memory of Johnny Cash] HARLECH/2006/WWB

You're the nearest thing to Xanadu, it's true,
a mystery of gleaming dreams and dew
descending to my side
where night may touch, confide,
you're the nearest thing to Xanadu, it's true.

You're the nearest thing to heaven on a plate,
a banquet for my flesh to satiate.
All-scenting tangibles
to suck-sing madrigals.
You're the nearest thing to heaven on a plate.

You're the ocean and the sky where I'm at sea.
Your downpour is a drenching symphony
where water music plays
to steer, herd holy lays,
you're the ocean and the sky where I'm at sea.

You're the backdrop from a storm of shooting stars,
a Venus foil of sweets and gleaming Mars.
Make battle peace with me,
war both our worlds to see
you're the backdrop from a storm of shooting stars.

2006 ODE ON A GREEK VASE
[Insp by 'Ode on a Grecian Urn' John Keats] PANTOUMS/2007

Oh happy love conveyed in a Greek vase,
cupped as the souvenir contained a prize.
I was your Venus and you were my Mars,
just moon-crossed lovers hand-locked by star rise.

Cupped as the souvenir contained a prize,
I stood, an open platter, ripe with fruit.
Just moon-crossed lovers hand-locked by star rise,
for toy soldiers march-danced to our suit.

I stood, an open platter ripe with fruit:
for photographs of storks' nests bred and flown;
for toy soldiers march-danced to our suit.
We wished a destiny as yet unknown.

For photographs of storks' nests bred and flown,
no mortal melodies contained pure arts.
We wished a destiny as yet unknown,
full-ripe with love, we played bold lovers' parts.

No mortal melodies contained pure arts,
though truth is beauty, beauty truth, to bear.
Full-ripe with love, we played bold lovers' parts;
pitched fertile carafe birthed at home, to share.

Though truth is beauty, beauty truth, to bear -
I was your Venus and you were my Mars.
Pitched fertile carafe birthed at home, to share.
Oh happy love, conveyed in a Greek vase.

2006 DING DONG PINK IT'S MATINS

[Insp by John Betjeman] QL (Comm)/2008-02; SALVADOR/2008/IDP

Oh my darling, how unseemly,
where your slacks are thinly sheening,
such a pertly pinkly backside
when you're dressed to sidely mount-ride.

Oh my lovely, kiss and cuddly,
now my palms are sticky, muddly,
thinking of your tennis elbow
and your ding dong arms, so noble.

Oh my, kiss and tell me, tickly
when those strident bells gong thickly.
What a wicked feather duster
when my truncheon fails its muster.

2006 PLOUGHING A FURROW
Tips/2006-09; PANTOUMS/2007/WWB

I love you like the earth,
bald sand and clay and chalk.
No need to speak of worth,
nor how to soar past talk.

Bold sand and clay and chalk;
none murmurs for bare flesh,
nor how to soar past talk,
sunk in deep planting's mesh.

None murmurs for bare flesh,
while plough and till suffice.
Sunk in deep planting's mesh,
my bloom scents soft pink spice.

While plough and till suffice
to clod my welcome soil,
my bloom scents soft pink spice,
pricked to rewards of toil.

To clod my welcome soil,
no need to speak of worth.
Pricked to rewards of toil,
I love you like the earth.

2006 PASSIONATE EMBRACE
PANTOUMS/2007/WWB

Let me love you with a passion,
let me shout it to the hillside.
Let me mould you to my fashion
like a saddle horse to hard-ride.

Let me shout it to the hillside,
while your whimsy's in the valley;
like a saddle horse to hard-ride
where no notch will keep a tally.

While your whimsy's in the valley,
broken gallop-bridge to gully,
where no notch will keep a tally
when my saddle-sore is fully

broken gallop, bridge to gully,
in your cup where I will dally
when my saddle-sore is fully
mounted in the arms of Sally.

In your cup where I will dally
let me mould you to my fashion.
Mounted in the arms of Sally
let me love you with a passion.

2007 CRUISING IN NEUTRAL
Tips/2007-09

Cruise to the most romantic day
to dine where candles flame away
in waxen passion, glowing dark,
yet shimmying and ever stark.

Stained eyes, set jellies, wobbling slow,
whenever love turns lights down low
and mouths a kiss of silent lark,
yet shimmying and ever stark.

Such playground games net bouncing balls,
to mould smooth gear when shrill time calls.
We, neutral, wordless, score chalk's mark,
yet shimmying and ever stark.

We share the silence of child-noise,
as Valentines no flame destroys.
Impassioned, cruising wick-hearts park,
yet shimmying and ever stark.

2006 SATISFACTION
Rejections Pile/2007/WWB

Sometimes slowly,
throbbing dull as thoughts in deep-breathed night.
Lightly first, caressing like the brush of leaves,
of linking pen and print
to sink in urgent movement,
thrashing limbs of trees into a gale; scribbled
before the sweat turns stale.
A sigh of sparklers exhaled into heaven.

Sometimes teasing,
giggling, plaiting fingertips
beneath the linen tablecloth and stain to red wine rings.
Where knives and forks trill feather-scraping orchestra
and every gentle probe's a scream
for more and more – more form, more lace,
a negligee of flesh, of skin,
of tingling to embroidered screams; undone.

Sometimes hard as prunes,
to spoon, to loose, to squeeze and juice
and work into a sweat of semolina
cold as parchment on the fridge.
A rigid calligraphic quill
to dip, to fill, to scratch into splodged worlds
and then to spill too late, too soon; so empty
as an inkwell on a slammed desk, obsolete.

Sometimes, always. Please;
and never stop, the thrill of wild applause.
A handshake, cup, or digital flash,
my flesh splashed on the page; between the sheets
and more, don't stop. Rage, plunge and pound;
my ground's a feet of ceilings thrust to stars.
A damp of creasing palms, of sunset glow,
basking with the novel, sated, dumped; beside a Mediterranean pool.

2007 THE PRIME OF SAMSON

Sarasvati/Issue 10/2010-05

I choose no fleur-de-lis with coy distracting smile
to taste my love upon your skin,
dividing where all roads leave absent
autumn grief.

I trace the burnished sunshine in a cup,
to pour your love from the smallest curling of your toe
into the nape of your footprint, where it leaves
no trace of green fresh shoots on sand.
Where petals wash your heel and climb your leg
to brushing hair that's never seen a razor's scrape;
unmanned as Samson in the harem of two pillars,
shorn like forest trunks.

I shave your prime into a trumpet's cock,
to breathe and raise all heaven on a note
of hammer hooded to the blast of spring
in April showers climbing Morning Glory.

Shiver into slumber of a dull day, firm and close
as petticoats of Colman's spooned to serve
the tickle on a rump and small of back;
where your spine stems as proud and fiercely pert
as cock robin in a garden shooting stars,
to dance in time to music, spheres.
Where chest and shoulders heave and plough a line
pooling straight as rain drips gold in grass.
Such full-fat butter dribbling down a chin,
to marching bands and troops of reds and greens.

Apollo's lips are in your stubble growth
and breathing dances through your hair, your skull,
to fleur-de-lis your brain in gentle sex
of all creation's golden daffodils.

2007 SHALL I COMPARE YOU?
From Newcastle to Malta/2009/WWB

It was not in winter, cheated of love
ripe scents, and outdoor food, when I met you.
Nor autumn's failure, budding yet untrue
as broken horseshoe's gutter, vowed above.

It was not in the springtime of soft skin,
nor overripe, where wasps have had their fill
of Adam's apple snaking Eve to thrills
beyond her homely figs, their pith and spin.

It was not a brief affair of secret dates,
of fattened letters, ribbon-tied and kept
when, from the bridges' dust and ashes, swept
long faithfulness of Madison County; late.

It was no loneliness of ironing shirts,
nor perfect prattling girls in Barbie skirts.

2008 IF YOU MUST LOVE ME
[Insp by 'If thou must love me' Elizabeth Barrett Browning]
A Mermaid's Tale/ Spring 2008; United Press 'Togetherness'

Oh, love me like the ever-flowing tide,
it laughs and cries and loves and smiles all day
in every fickle womanly sweet way
and yet its night is dark and broad and wide.

It tumbles to a thousand fancies, yet
by tricking and by teases, fun will last
when pleasantries and frumperies are past.
So by such changes, sun will never set.

Love all my nothings, then you'll never mind,
except the price of tissue-mountain heights.
If I am dry, please wet me – till you find
your creature comforts rage like Blackpool lights.
Love me while love's tides rage before, behind;
for oceans lee and lie in sailing's sights.

2007 FROM THE HEART 2
[Insp by 'From the Heart' Pamela Trudie Hodge] Tips 80/2010-12

When I wrote a poem for my husband
on his birthday; on Valentine's Day; on our Anniversary
in December—as the world celebrated snow and cake,
he did not understand it: whether it rhymed or not,
was brilliant or mundane, publishable or memorable.

He read the picture, scanned cheap standard phrases
and ate the cake I made him: moist and sweet, full of love.
He could estimate the logistics of a wife:
flowers, cards, chocolates, endless declarations of devotion.
Dry-eyed, I wrote him a poem.

Yet he was there when our son was born;
could measure placental size
overflowing the kidney dish.
Forgot flowers for our second-born, in subdued light;
held my hand; brought in fresh nightie and miniature clothes;
gave baby a cuddly toy; matching big brother's.

My husband's not a poet, but his word-picture made me cry
that day, when he held our third son, brightly-lit in special care:
a flimsy photograph.

The original was carried in the darkroom of his arms
as he tucked him in unprocessed, with Rusty Rabbit;
his black suit a fragile negative.

2011 AFTER RAIN
2011/05/PUBLD, Reach/Feb 12

I will not sit in the garden today,
watch lonely sunset, just like yesterday.
The heavens have opened up; full of shine
like when you smile and I know that you're mine.

I will walk among flowers brushed with rain
and now, the light on leaves drive me insane
to have you home. The clouds have vaporised
above the scenting stock; I feel alive.

2008/080 MY LOVE
Crystal/2010-03

I love you like the sea, my dear,
for it is very wet
and I love you like the sand, my dear,
though it is very dry.

I love you, Cornish, like ice cream,
for it is creamy, sweet
and I love you, homely Welsh cakes,
all plain and very filling.

I love you when the world is dark,
though you're not very light
and I love you when your tuneful snore
keeps my love wide awake.

I'll love you when my wrinkles map
the rub of life and love
and then I'll have a rest, my dear,
while harps pluck memories.

2008 EROS OF THE MUSE (*Tips/Spring 2009*)

He comes with night and morning's shining wings,
descends on Psyche, prone, where he alights.
She turns her gaze as air, ethereal, sings
and wraps her love in feather-down delights.

He rises, harsh and strong; she's weak with love
and cannot break the rhythm of his flow.
She pants and pulls him closer, from above,
refracting gleams as godhead/darkness show.

She grieves before his leaving mould and stamp
of impotent weak arms around broad chest.
He heaves to absence morning's cold and damp
as she rolls into dreams; knows that he's gone.

But not for long; all day drags, dimming sheen
into her night, as sunshine brims serene.

2008 THREADS OF DESTINY 2

[Insp by Claire Knight/Metverse Muse, March 2008]
Metverse Muse, India/Issues 29-31/2012-05

I can web a sight of true love
leaning on the evening air,
where a BBQ is sizzling
and light giggles grow to stare.
Of the balmy chill of nightfall
as we all adjourn indoors
and your green eyes keep sky dancing
into future's bright contours.

I can thread those winding street signs,
that each lunchtime winds you in
to my loving arms and blushes,
where your thoroughfare will win.
To brush of hands along a path,
spun to gossamer's pure silk,
in the bloom of a walled garden
where sweet refreshings taste as milk.

I can weave our missed encounters,
like the stars that ever shine.
So golden – our eternity –
as seasons migrate in line.
Bliss of Adam's chance encounter,
Eve's art lights her garden's spark
with knight-steel and anvil fruiting
star-seed webs in dawn-frost park.

2009 TAKE ME TO PARADISE

[Insp by 'A Time of Knowing' Claire Knight/Reach, June/July 2009]
Quantum Leap, 1st Prize Open Comp/2018-05/PUBLD

You will not be jealous if I say
love rests between my sensual thighs
in wave on wave of nectar on the rose,
that, having risen well, cannot lie down,
nor droop, nor wilt and fall.

You will not be jealous of my love
that rests in sated pleasure, like the bee
that dozes in the sun, quite drunk with sky
and buffs the gentle meadow where he lays
prone as Cupid's bow.

You will not be jealous if you find
that I know well how great the magnitude
of love sails round Cape Horn; to pleasure air;
nor how lightly love sails in a day,
when all the world's a storm.

And I'm so sure of sand and tide
to bladderwrack my days
on some stray island, where
the turtles stone
with jealousy of age, where love rocks

me to sleep, in depths before each shore.
But though you green a little, the butterfly
is buffed on sands of time and more:
the lifeguard ripples muscles,
time to flag - a love, a Paradise; a sandy shore.

2009 RUSSIAN RING

(United Press 'A Piece of my Heart'/2011; Star Tips/May 2011)

There is no greater gift we can receive
in all of life and close relationships,
than, when we leave, friends know that we bequeath
our own true self, a prize that then equips
a wider circle of companion rings:
to live when we have gone. Our gift is love,
blooms long in memory and, well-known, sings
like freshest birdsong's nesting from above.
Like Russian rings, connections link through years
of childhood, young romance, lost dreams and plans;
all interlocking through each friendship's tears,
yet one ring brushing palms of loving strands.
The gift of love's a gold band that confirms
unique encircling links our life affirms.

2008 COLOURS OF LOVING
(Poets' names; with variations)

This is how I love you,   (…Poe loves you,)
let me tell the ways
that Gray can say, without bright blushing,
or removing stays.

I love Pope red, I love Keats blue
like prickly roses bathed in dew.

I love your words worth morning yellow
sunbeams on Blake hair,   (..bleak hair,)
and bouncing lovely, most unseemly
golf balls in green star   (Tennis on green, bare.)

I love you purple, love dun pink
but not inside white bathroom sink.   (..Dark Dylan's sink.)
And though a shower's silver lining
tickles rump insane   (tickles Baudelaire,)
your blissful sleeping cow-purse hurry
gurgles 'Erbert's drain.   (Gurgles down dark lair.)

I love your brandy whiskey rum   (..randy whiskered tum)
and throaty voice when you, dear, come   (..Motion's come.)

I love Shake Speares in moonlit shadows
of flat screen TV,
when Burns' last sticky, sweet-scent Rolo's
swallowed; inside me.   (..Hannah's fee.)

I love you spruce and sharp and fine   (..you puce and Smartie faun)
and grow in love each time you whine.   (..in girth each time we dine.)

This is how I Hop kins' Bridges,   (..I love you mellow,)
Burn-side to a broad,
by Swim-Burn dowse-date Larkin' gazing (..-ing dowse-days. Midges)
 where turquoise midnights ford.   (Where memories are stored.)

I love your prison-chiselled cell,   (…you prismed where I sail,)
To court in Poole, banged up but well
                      (in storm or flood or howling gale.)

2008 RETROSPECTIVE
Paradise Lost/2009; United Press/National Poetry Anthology 2010

If I had known, back then, how fruit tastes now,
skirts berthed to billow white and cloud your brow:
not decked with gentle ageing, if we stay
together, now as then, in every way.

Nor with that shock a groom would race to grieve,
if his own runaway bride could choose to leave.
Pause on some Sistine breath, exhaling life,
discerning flaming swords to Paradise.

My fenders and your springs moor painful creeds
that glister sunset reach, bend Norfolk's reeds.
Can I tack lengthened shadows, slanting past,
or flush to changing seasons falling fast?

If I had known you now, me then, what thatch
would cottage love buoyed far from broad-sail's hatch?

2009 THE KEY SENT
Star Tips (135)/2020-01

Round paths crossed many times before feet met,
like loving moments tripped into a dream
of shifting features which had not yet set
into a face beloved, where hearts had room
to grow much greater love than all loves seem.
Once in a lifetime, love can bud and bloom

to floribundas of delight that please
a pilgrim heart to touch, to kiss, to meet
that other self where matches strike to tease
sweet Juliet, who's ripe to kiss, to see
her Romeo, whose love brings willing feet
where crushing sweet aromas turn the key.

Once in a lifetime, love can bud and bloom,
where crushing sweet aromas turn the key.

2009 ONLY A MAN
'And Again Last Night'/2009/IDP

Although he was only a man, and a woman must always be right,
he arrived home a little earlier than usual:
briefcase, tie and papers dumped
to ease himself into that comfortable sofa and feel for ice,
for thrill, for any little signs that men always miss
like hair or clothes or tidy homes or food.
All could wait the fiery bouquet
disposed of, promptly, in her arms; like a baby.
He had to try extra hard tonight, for he was only a man
and a woman must always be right,
especially when there was no last night, nor the night before.
The risk of failure was sufficient to chill his manhood,
like sea-bathing at Easter.
Her smile and kiss encouraged him, a little.
His trump card? A CD, female vocalist; award-winner.
Too much to ask for poetry; for bardic expressions of lust,
for a woman is always right when the words are wrong
and roses are not blooming but consumed too late for Valentines.
A long slow comfortable pancake or three later,
endorphins happy as Jaffa cakes and squirty cream for the young;
tart as lemons and waist-sprinkling sugar for the old;
it was time to ease the belt; slob out over TV.
Dispose of practical hindrances; like children, bra-straps, women's moods,
to blow teasing kisses, for he was only a man standing attention,
far too keen and eager for warmth and comforting food
and the instant gratification of a woman who has stopped talking.
Downstairs, a woman must always be right when he dallies awhile, creaks upstairs,
wondering if he's done enough, for his well-watered bouquet to bloom.
He makes quite certain she is nothing but moans; to leap triumphant,
score as he may a second time, in every which way while that scent
of love bouquets to marital strife to die for.
He was only a man ... and again last night, she was only a woman.

2009 TO HAVE AND TO HOLD
Tips 80/2010-05

Awkwardly reading pictures, prices,
to blushing at the counter, where a girl
just 18 years old, politely asked
if she could assist in purchasing,
or offering to show the range, the size.

Her own hands were a pattern of the years
of pushing prams, of laundry, wear and tear;
all stubby, naked, bleached to racing hearts
of 18 years before, when he first came
inside her awkwardness and blushing glance.
To have and have quite well, through all those years
that life had throbbed with hardness, pain and joy.

Shamefaced, she could not ask, but he had words
to pose perplexity as simple need
that he could kiss away with card and pin,
if only she dared to say, I do, again
A perfect match, eternalised by gold,
expanding to her digits, girth; his words
engraved in 'I love you'.
                                   It fitted well.

A leitmotif that needed neither church nor blessing.
I do, she said, and left that superstore,
a wedding band expanding to her girth
of pristine love, that shouted to the world:
he loves this menopausal blushing bride
and pays the price again, performing - as a groom -
actions that show he won't be needing
any replacement.

2009 BOX ROOM
Salopeot/Issue 144/Summer 2012

He painted blue
and I don't know how we could choose
to match that shade of cymbals loud
and true.

He brushed all day
and rollered all four walls, and edged
until the dinner bell took words
away.

And then my look
across poured wine glass, vivid red,
(that spoke of hours in the sunset) shook.

He glossed over
stroke by careful stroke; softly done.
I made the bed, spreading out creased
cover.

2011 KOH-I-NOOR
Crystal/Jan 15? Malawi reading/Apr 13

It must be said, he is the best there is,
a diamond, many-faceted and hard,
and I say nothing lightly, even this.
He's polished, gleaming, smooth; let's wear a placard,
... to make you envious like the stars that shine.
My husband is not less than Koh-i-noor
and you can't have him. Cut or whole, he's mine.
I wear him like a god; a woman; more,
a curse on all those houses, as they foil
misfortune's falls, for everyman's a poet
that wears a diadem of such great spoil.
The Tree of Life worms great as those that know it:
for brilliance disappoints, because it can,
though hardness is an asset in a man.

2011 I'M THE ONE
2019-11/PUBLD Star Tips 134

I'm the one, but do you love me,
sinking mermaids in your hair?
Lapping, bathing in your shoulder.
Tell me, are you really there?

I'm the one, but do you need my
sandy arms and flooding tide,
wrapping safe within my shoreline,
where your ocean may have died.

I'm the one, but can I love you
like the seasons, like the sea?
Does your ebb and flow and sunshine
overwhelm and soften me?

I'm the one, but can I want your
drownings in the fickle tide?
There my footprints always vanish,
while your arms are open wide.

Are we beached on the same island?
Are you drifting; are you gone?
I'm here, and yet I'm waiting.
Surely, drowning love's not wrong.

2009 AH! SUNFLOWER
Tips 75/2010-01/PUBLD

Ah, Sunflower, weary traveller in time,
you have no sore feet nor strained neck in the sun.
You seek out Apollo, the Globe is a crime
of necking and straining, until the film's done.

Youth wears pine fresh, all lynx, weak with desire,
inflamed by virgin dress, ghouls Goth as snow.
For knightly they arise, all mail, aspire
like sunflowers, wherever they wish to go.

2011 A DREAM WITHIN A DREAM
[Insp by Edgar Allan Poe] Dawntreader (46) 2019-03

Take this kiss as we hold hands
and wander through the springtime plants
that spread forever here.

Is this a dream, please hold me taut
as if it is the darkest night
and then hold me some more.

The birds are singing in the trees
and I can't see them darting, place
my lead-in further on.

It is a dream, I hope to tail
where angel dresses dance and play
narcissus' every shade.

Will it be gone before we stile
beyond this breath's eternity,
for heaven rests with ease

My ears roar and my heart beats fluster,
when will I shore, will it all last
past trampled grains of sand?

Please take my hand, like pilgrims, pale,
my naked grasp won't fly away
where silence, weeping, goes.

My life, like grains of sand, like stars,
how can we, love, for this rehearse?
O God! I grasp some more.

I am not waving, but drowning near,
I dream within my dream, and how
it seems like we could touch.

2011 SWEET SIXTEEN

*[Insp by Margaret Whitaker 'Letting down summer dresses'] Star Tips
119/2017-05*

There is a time for every season
under heaven,
but not above.

And I remember now, just sweet 16,
the age when, so grown up, you'd stay out late
or play your MP3, watch loud TV,
and take a clutch of GCSEs, and then
to college, Uni, apprenticeships, the world
your oyster.

There are no clothes to let down,
so very let down, to watch you grow
and see what colour were those eyes?
And all you'd know, and what you'd choose.
Your personality, your interests, tastes
in food? In culture? In daily pains of youth.

So much to say, so much to do
and would you have needed DLA
Wheelchair-bound, or lifelong care?
It's not there anywhere, for me to know
and I can't show the world just how you grew;
what school you went to, how long you grew your hair.

I only know one thing, down fine and dark
as your father's.
Oh, and another thing, you looked – oh –
so much like your little brother.
Except, you were so young to die
and I will never know the colour of your eyes.
So young to die
                    that day, that hour, that moment
before you were born.

2009 18 YEARS
Poetry Rivals 'The Rhythms of Life'/2010-12

It is a truth universally acknowledged that a woman of independent
means
is not in need of a husband nowadays
and that a married man lives longer
or so it seems,
so when anyone mentions marriage, even a happy marriage,
no woman would respond with neutrality.
The happy will congratulate
the sad will commiserate
and all want to know the length of sentence.
So when a man, escaping a fate worse than death,
marries a woman escaping the dustiest shelf-death or worse,
it is entirely a match made in heaven
or hell.
When mentioning an anniversary, some will crush with humour
or last word,
while the man has not begun his sentence
though he may remain a man
or free.
So celebrating every year, like paradisal clockwork:
where chocolates, flowers, cards and meals progress
like night and day of angels round the throne
and Love Lies Bleeding only streaming birth
and birdsong
like the lark or nightingale,
with Cristalino's Metodo Tradicional Reserva
from Jaume Serra, in España,
two glasses chink and vow another eighteen years
and hope the young will remember/mirror/pay, if fate allows
another Cava reflecting loving years,
for still or sparkling, they are a lovely couple.

2013 WHAT'S IN A NAME?
Quantum Leap (78)/2017-05

It is a regal name, that face
is more familiar than my skin.
And though it ages fast, and grows
away from that I first saw – yet
it's oh, so there, and present, and the best
that any face could be.
A wealth of lines now spread
to greet each autumn,
though we have fall enough
and then some more.
It is sufficient on the road, we still
-like children- hold hands
in the darkening wood.
Oh, read no fortune to us now,
for we had crowns and kingdoms in the past
and do not sing to death the mermaid, sinking
beneath the waves, beyond the town, off Cromer
pier. There is a prosperous land too,
where fishes swim and pearl those eyes
of seeing.
So if I had to choose a name like Edward,
think none of these are worthy of my love.
A guardian and protector he remains,
and may our flesh and bones melt to that marrow
of earth to earth; that place our hearts are buried,
together there, where birds spring through the trees,
with blossom for our pillows and our clouds.
So sleep me to the last, where dreams are ended,
for there's no better face to quell all tears.

2011 LOVE FOR SALE
Star Tips 111/2016-01

It's been a weird day, so I'll go gently,
though not into that good night, that's so absent.
The silence is now dying, fundamentally,
with Juliet. She's leaning through the casement:
the dark is rising. Trick or Treat's abroad,
and how she sighs for Romeo to come home.
They need hard cash and all they can afford
is gum and alcopops. They're so alone!
Their love is true, to die for, how they'll haunt
their parents' courtyard, till they're given wings.
They must elope to Mantua, to flaunt
their love (by trade, or children); other things
that are beyond love's story, and would fail
to rouse our sympathy, when grief's for sale.

2011 AND NOW MY LIFE IS...
[Insp by Tichborne's Elegy, 1586]; Aspire/2012-04

My life is full of blooms, each gift so full.
My days are rich with sweets, they melt so fast.
My wine is poured, when will there be some more?
And all the days are years and they have passed.
The glass is now half empty and half full
and now the day is done, and more will pass.

Your life is full of youth, and what of cares?
Your days are rich with verve, they are your own.
Your wine is barely corked, when will it pour?
And all the years are days, and they remain.
The glass is so full now, I empty fast
and now the hour has come, for it will pass.

Our life is one day in the year, for love.
Our days are rich with absence, hour by hour.
This wine is poured out, heady, full of cares
and all the hours are dregs, while yours ferment.
The glass is smashed so soon, and yours brand new
and now the moment's past, for you're mature.

2012 LATE AFTERNOON
Star Tips (130)/2019-03

You do not read my words. What should I write?
When we can take a Mazda for a spin
and, of necessity, you let me in
the driver's seat. Then clutch the door in fright.
You walk so fast, oblivious of the scenes
that zoom and focus, pan or tilt, and yet
my mind's your everyday and in those dreams
that keep you comatose. You so forget
to pause at photographs, or share the vast
indoors. A picnic table in the sun:
a naughty treat, a healthful drink, the past
gathers steam and motion; then it's gone.
You surf, read, doze, relax; I act and play,
returning to your arms' breadth end of day.

2013 JUNE BIRTHDAY
Grief that's always dying/WWB2013-11

It did not seem quite promising, at first:
the man was wide awake; in biking gear
and in the garage before I opened an eye
to stagger scenes of day. To celebrate
a birthday, new as every year from now,
the date there would be no card from our son...
not this one – busy with exams – nor then
the other, safely tucked up, far away.
What changes cuckooed trembling in the branches?
A new day dawning when it was so old,
as wood and stone and earth and vacant flowers?
Precipitating morning's ugly drop
from safe routines; the place for cards and gifts...
and just enough of time to drain a cup
of strong dark coffee; rummaging through breakfast
parcels; and those cards the postman brought.
All gone. It seemed like nothing remained the same,
in wracking sobs that dowsed no candle; lit
simply in my heart and in my head.
The day progressed through chores, and words online,
until the urge to kick the pricks, and travel
to congregations of bedding plants, all blooming.
Returning to the trowel and pricking out.
The new year dawned, fresh-tyred and fit for purpose,
and so the day's pale ending planted hope:
a table at Pinocchio's, for three;
Italian waiter; salad/pasta/wine,
with love as red as poured out life, and joy
that a teen could say (not think!) we were 20 years
younger than, er, sometime; and, oh, how sweet,
a mum and dad could eat; and still hold hands.

2015 MY LOVE IS LIKE A HOT TUB
Star Tips (111) 2016-01

Haze lays beneath the hills at Ambleside,
where coffee tasted bitter and so sour.
Walking beside Rydal Water, weakness tried
to find the new athletic me's spent power.

A walk in the park – as hope vaporised –
limping for England; never mind the view.
Spring drifts of solitude materialised,
aching on that inward eye, it's true.

I gave up hope beside the Autumn bed,
sipping and wrinkling up to bitter dregs.
My love persuaded: striding on ahead,
bringing soft shoes, fresh Meds, and wheels for legs.

A hot tub in the great outdoors is fine,
canoodling with my love, just 'cos he's mine.

2016 SILVER ANNIVERSARY
Reach (221) 2017-02

I thought that silver was to be loved-up,
a ring/a necklace/champagne/family round,
a sign of drinking bitter dregs – the cup –
those best years now downhill and all aground.

I thought to stroke a balding silver pate,
to hold that bony fist – a claw – and wish
my father's gentlest sleep to death's sweet plate
and grief to pass with Noël's late winter dish.

I think of fizzing glass and silvered tree;
a man sat in his chair, who – patient – waits
brief kissing hugs from the daughter that is me,
distracted, where a groom's love compensates

The moonrise from a bride of long ago;
a father's golden sunset, fading slow.

2016 AUTUMN FOLLOWS SPRING
Dial 174 (111) 2017-09

If I were to leave you
it would not be for another;
for men are fickle, weak and always follow
their hearts, their plans and mounting appetites.

If I were to leave you,
it would not be for dreams;
I had them all with you, it now appears
that nights will blaze to sunset in a while.
If I were to leave you,
it would not be wild fancy life's experience
in books, on TV screens, or Cyber-dating,
nor friendship, music, poetry, nor wine.

A different age/ or childhood/ values/ culture
could bouquet chance, or gender, family life,
to bloom and fade in myrrh of no tomorrow
beyond horizons of a different stage

If I were to leave you
it would not spring from love, though love is death;
a poet's pining is too much Adonis
and you have given and received it all.
If I would leaving leaving ever leave you
finally forever like the tide,
wild fickle blazing sunset faints and shades, dear,
grimly reaping grief of endless loss.

2017 FAIREST OF THE SEXES
Star Tips (129) 2019-01

There is a time when woman changes minds,
to flit and flight with wining/dining, friends,
or clubs/societies/trips, and then man finds
that nothing he can do may make amends.

Man likes to win and woo and settle down,
his slippers well tucked in, he's so at home.
He rarely plays away/or like a clown.
Relaxing well; thinks that no day will come

When she moves out/on/off beyond his dinner,
to find a peace/or fun/attention/youth.
If he had wooed too little – who's the sinner?
Every day and hour she needed truth.

A man who's ruled his kingdom well, waits love,
a woman's peace is his, or, God above…!

2017 LAKES/BIRTHDAY AMBLE
Crystal (103) 2018-01

The scenes are all of sunsets in their shine,
of whitest stars – like sheep – that frame or glow
Herdwick nights or boat-brights brimming wine
to sip or swallow hazily and slow.

They're perfectly at rest to capture space,
the warmth of home, without that hard-won climb –
twelve months' peaceful moments in time's race
and whispered breaths of clouds dripped into rhyme.

To mark impending summits with a view,
he strides, lens poised, up Stock Ghyll's Giggling Goose;
she downs a pint (no, half), feels old. This new
life-phase crashes in without a choice.

Autumn/winter, sunset/sunrise break,
promenade retirement wide awake.

2017 LATE PLANS
Crystal (103) 2018-01

I do not say you should have children late,
although life's choices may have flown like sand:
in a desert/wind-storm/simply unplanned.
How long – that man of dreams – how long to wait?

Life passes, fully lived, until that state
we almost missed. A man holds out his hand
with gifts and promises... that magic wand
of love, that piles the future on his plate.

First date (the wife recalls), 'He had a yacht.'
'I had to buy a boat,' he laughs, accounts.
'You said, "Come meet the parents." Well, so what?
I never thought that gesture – wow – amounts...'

To wedding bells, to children and, once they've grown:
old age/retirement/listening for a phone.

2017 BEAUTY SPOT
Star Tips (135) 2020-01

Nowhere. It is true; though it's not yours
and mine is samely different in its place.
If I have never sent it there, but here,
True love must search all earth like Psyche's wraith.

There is a spot, it's true, no beauty spot
more perfect nor divine (specially mine).
Enjoyable and countless are the moments,
if I needed to justify my place a jot.

Perfection's fickle, logical as breath,
so you may raise a mountain up unmoved.
Clouds parted while you looked another way;
beatific was the sight yours found for you.

My spot's the corner of my loved one's eyes;
nowhere else; what I can see, you can't.

2017 LOVE'S PACE
Quantum Leap (83)/2018-08

My love, he's like a hurricane: that's slow
to take offence/arrive or leave, I find
his fame's renowned for days and days. To show,
when he arrives at last, just turns me blind.

To take offence: arrive or leave. I find
he's neither more nor less, but just himself
when he arrives, at last! Just turns me blind,
I nearly –almost- was left on the shelf.

He's neither more nor less, but just himself:
a treasure dumped by crueller eyes than mine.
I nearly (almost) was left on the shelf;
such value that I've gained by lightning sign.

A treasure dumped by crueller eyes than mine.
None tuned into his frequency like me
Such value – what I've gained. By lightening sign,
he is my weather all-ways he can be.

None tuned into his frequency like me…
his fame's renowned for days and days, to show
he is my weather always. He can be
my love. He's like a hurricane that's slow.

2018 CELEBRATING
Star Tips/2020-01

Generously reduced holiday cottage in Devon,
last-minute, considering imponderables.
No foreign travel: sunshine-scorched UK.
Storms threatened on the moors.

Tomatoes ripening in the lean-to greenhouse:
starved of moisture morning and night,
in need of respite; oases; mirages.
Son home from Uni, post-Dissertation.

Proving love and nurturing (fed and watered),
we contemplated chances of DIY/
painting/repairing/brief outings.
Devon hung like a dragonfly on a rising stem.

We laughed/delayed/enjoyed moments of calm,
mesmerised by hours of sleep-thrilled youth.
Brief encounters at the mid-point between
breakfast (his) and unconsciousness (ours).

Generously refreshed to hit the town (library),
barely voicing parental advice;
meds sorted; deadlines; re-sit.
Winds dried and we rose above our pond.

Iridescent with hope when pen hit paper
(bum hit seat; digits/iPad),
we scoured Norfolk for homely Postbridge,
expansive Plymouth, vibrant Tavy

Watching sails; or downing tea;
How Hill/Horsey Mere (as damselflies, or swallowtails);
Thetford the motte and bailey of nowhere.
We stayed awake past midnight – deadlines strayed dreams.

Like Pooh-sticks, we released all Devon phantoms.
Summer danced as we booked a posh hotel:
returned son to final clear-out of digs, pending…
celebrating in style with Macdonald Ansty. Coventry.

2018 PROSTRATE FOR MORSELS?
Reach/2018-09

Yesterday, all my phantoms fleshed in everything
that's unimaginable on a Bank Holiday.
Yesterday, it was unfathomable and full of pain,
though what the purpose/meaning/life
in backwaters of pure pleasure, pain or past?
Yesterday, the Building Inspector – due to call –
failed again; I filled my waiting time with flowers.
A florabundance of aching back/strained knees,
until she phoned with wizard words:
our magic carpet approved; we flew.
Yesterday, hospital appointment to support
my love, my life, my all; and, this gets hard,
a cache of tests and flexi-camera
reaching parts unmentionable (males present).
Failing to claim territorial rights
(except for Sudoku and Solitaire),
the young female doctor saw it all…
beyond my wildest dreams; or yours.
Yesterday, they found an answer (not for wimpish
men): how operations reach the parts
you never want to hear, without fermented grape,
or hopping in waiting room, pint in hand.
So now I say, Yesterday
all his troubles dosed with meds.
Today? CT Scan, non-urgent; six-month wait
to morcellate beyond nightmare.
Set down
this. Set down
this. Crowds flowed over Waterloo Bridge/
the Thames beneath.
Tomorrow, flowing like the Red Sea (men everywhere):
non-cancerous prostate better/worse than feared.
Yesterday, rounding off with folk music,
downing pint of cider; contemplating love:
I genuflect against erectile dysfunction…
tomorrow.

MOTHER'S DAY 2018
Star Tips/2020-03

So many things I want for Mother's Day:
and most of them impossible to see.
My husband's only solace is to pray
he pulls it off with fine temerity.

I must say first, all ladies receive gifts
of blooming daffodils in church. The young
may fail to grasp how much each smile uplifts,
nor why mums (crying) are so highly strung.

A card (on time); a phone call; chocs; warm blooms;
and Sunday lunch/or outing/treats well-planned.
Can all women grieve the cold of empty rooms,
grave petals fading when they are unmanned?

Simplicity – like dads – it does not matter;
except to hear their voice, or pitter-patter.

2018 COMING OF AGE
Star Tips 126/2018-06

One day I will learn how little a card matters
when all of nature lies exhausted before me.
One day I will learn that improvised meals are best,
flung together with brash love and family time.
One day I will not care how you wash/dress/graze food
like browsing online for chill out that vanishes.
One day all my skies will be yours to ponder on;
my garden florabundance will fade and bloom in verse;
one day my breath will be carried by wind and river,
my love only an oasis in your memory.
One day, my son or daughter/they (what you prefer),
will know the depths of mother's love; and father's too.
I wish them life and health and breath, and space to be.
Less clamour in the mind, just peace. One day.

2018 WAKE UP, MISSUS
Star Tips Xtra/May 2021

Last night I dreamed
myself mistress of Trump:
He gave me posh clothes/skirts to wear,
so I shook hands with footballers
and other six-packs.
Woke up, groggy, disorientated,
thanking my lucky stars
no X-Ratings of marital bliss.

Took the bus to Wroxham,
downed a pint of Aspall's:
purifying those parts
my dream – thankfully – didn't reach.
Numbed me to most things:
life/family/moments.

Reading poetry beside the river,
hoping for a doctor (any Doctor)
tonight…

2018 GUNTON HALL
Reach (Issue 243) 2018-12

I felt a dizzy, haze fuelled by pink gin,
with strawberries floating on a peaceful sea,
as I read (late) my 238:
a tour-de-force by bus, last year.
My cocktail's laced with prosecco, bubble-light,
as man hopes for a walk that leaves me beached:
from Gunton Hall to Corton (pigs might fly).
although this mermaid seas the utter east,
to daisy chain my muses into brine.
One day – you'll find me yet – beyond these shores,
when Warners are less gone to youthful sighs.
My glass is almost empty – Autumn's slow –
I am the past (so long ago), once dead.
Tonight I dance and swallow one last berry.

2019 TOMORROWS
Star Tips 134/ 2019-11

I don't know where my youth has gone, where life
washed itself away down plughole. What
my soggy skin-buffed bubble fingers found
to drain the suds and debris of old plates.

My cups are chipped and housed in cupboard stacks;
all saucepans free from sauciness and scum.
Most glasses don't match now, the best have smashed
to star-shine on the lino of scratch broom.

Dense dust shreds carpets every time I clean,
like grey hairs that won't hide in gleam or shine.
The clock ticks less each year, as music fades,
discordant with tomorrow's tones of pain.

I live, I breathe, my joints can move me yet:
and so can prunes; and I'm not deep in debt.

2019 GRADUATED PARENTING
Reach (Issue 251)/2019-08

I hope you don't mind, son, just one last time,
your title –that first moment – 'It's a boy!'
When anaesthesia screamed too loud to mime,
'Please, does my baby live?' Demanding joy.

And then he wanted pull ups: pink, not blue,
and sparkly things; the stage; not muddy balls.
We graced you with acceptance, boldly true,
that parents' love could gaily mop up falls.

We prided in each aperture and shutter:
trophies of your selfhood graced our walls.
We supported you through dreams, and then that utter
place of Graduation. Fresh life calls.

And now your pain asks gender-neutral terms,
which love's ageing fifties parenting reaffirms.

2020 FIRST CLASS YORK

[Insp by Shell-Shock, Peter Geoffrey Paul Thompson, Reach 25])
Reach 2020-05; PERSEPHONE (Vol 2)/2021

To find some peace in rhythmic mile on mile,
deep-drinking wine in first class carriage seat
with long-time love, who's not been back awhile:
office commute, long-distance; what a treat.

For him? About the journey, getting there,
and playing hookie; no long boring meetings.
For her? The change of scene, all-glistering, where
pained family absence stokes dull-embered feelings.

Red/rosé, downed a treat, round Foss or Ouse:
he plays Sudoku, remembers the hard grind.
She contemplates the Hampton: nookie/loos.
Bright mesmerising sky lifts, to unwind

The cost of peopling earth with special moments.
Musing sun-scorched clouds Persephone opens.

2020 WAITROSE

Reach (Issue 267) 2020-12

Feel the joy of Cringleford by night:
sat in a car park beneath the sickle moon.
A bright light beaming like a natal star,
and slumbered thatched roof church, a stone's throw near.

Is it enough to love to sit and breathe?
Hospitals – the nationwide – can't promise this.
A picnic bench – such luxury – no coffee,
my Alpha One out hunting bottled gin.

To feel such comfort, walking down the Loke,
the horses put to bed/an oak tree felled.
Clinging – for dear life – to my lover's arm.
I feel I've earned a medal: I can walk!

Not Covid. Simple crick in neck gone haywire.
Raw pain's relief; forgetting to bring a mask.

2021 APPOINTED HOUR
Star Tips 144/2021-12

Beautiful day, sunshine in winter,
-snow forecast overnight-
for one day like no other,
since Covid/Lockdown 3/
the prospect of Valentine's Day at home.

Such joy, to rise so early,
get in the car,
drive a distance eyeing tarmac roads.
Trees bare, plain landscape all around,
the prospect – almost daily – of crocus beam.

We park the car, put on masks,
shiver in an early queue outside:
they're running late, it's already 8.45,
then in/hand sanitiser/check temperatures.
Bubble-sign and enter; sit, remove masks…

He's ready – in position – all kitted out.
In turn, we wear a visor: it steams and blurs,
discombobulated swap rooms for X-Ray.
Escaping soon – gripping chair for dear life
(that's cheap; an extra fiver for PPE).

'Just rinse out now.' Polishing manually,
(no use of aerosols – projecting virus).
We leave contented; 'See you next year.'
Morning coffee/health walk/garden centre:
Barely lunchtime. Overpoweringly full day.

2021 EMPTY GLASS
For the Many not the Few/Volume 23/2022-04/Amazon

TikTok, it's twelve o'clock,
sat in a garden bursting daffodils,
Hyacinth. Oh, yes. No?
The Malbec's glowing dreams of Tsunamis
and rules of six. Remember?
Easter gatherings unfurling downpours of hail.
Only the blackbird warns me of the worm.
It's shocking to contemplate black lives matter;
immoral to mention white daffs, hyacinths, or tinus viburnum.
My bloody wine spills, like orgasm,
so how can I consider midnight, or a moon?
Shocked 'About Face' – I haven't read it yet.
Mock me now:
my love/my life is vaccinating.
I'm home – alone:
the nightingale's in bed…
she's born to raise a Jew,
a grand-sire's mater,
in Spring, when all the world is breeding Summer.
The ants my playmates – hoping for KP.
I'm off to Mamma Mia/chocolate downtime,
to contemplate how my trans boy
                              became a girl.
Mock me – heaven – now.

2021 THURSDAY, AFTER
Crystal Issue 128/2022-03

The hard part of the waiting, yet again,
Good Friday – think low fibre, what to buy.
I dream of walking down a country lane.

On Saturday a Covid test, remain
at home, self-isolate, let nightmares lie.
The hard part of the waiting yet again.

No lamb on Easter Sunday, chocolates (plain),
enough (as cake or pasta, no red dye).
I dream of walking down a country lane.

On Wednesday next – in Lockdown – fluids drain.
Drive; leave him sedated; chill hours fly.
The hard part of the waiting yet again.

Hope colonoscopy will reacquaint
the doctor with rogue polyp. Cut! That site…
I dream of walking down a country lane.

His day procedure over, I'm insane,
benignly beg the universe, despite
the hard part of the waiting, yet again.
I dream of walking down a country lane.

2021 IF...
Star Tips (142) 2021-06

If I am unlucky,
succumb to diabetic stroke
or other imponderables post-2020,
I don't want to stare as dust-motes cover
my comfort zone of home's disordered mind,
nor watch as clutter piles, not put away.

Please put me in the garden in the sun,
with scene enough and shade to stir warm joy.
I promise not to leap up: weed or dig,
nor contemplate new changes/shrubs or flowers.
Oh, keep the wasp at bay, bring butterflies
to nectar my release in dreams long-gone.

If I am unlucky,
don't frown at my domestic goddess malapropisms,
nor berate my loving/mothering/50's childhood.
Only, give me your face. Your smile.

2021 ARCTIC BLAST

QL comp 2021-08 (Comm), Issue 95/2021-08

Arctic blast freckled windscreen,
scrape and shiver, early start.
Reversing off drive, the garden to die for,
strawberries and cream flourish the paving:
April's last fling into sunshine.

The waiting game – longing summer loungers,
sea and endless sky.
Leave him, drive home; park.
Go for a long walk of daffodil gardens,
interior redesigns and conifer removals.
Pass yellow jackets/cars/endless vaccine queues,
Stop for newspaper/chocolate/plants
and pass, socially distancing and neighbourly.

Dig, plant, dig, water.
Coffee's indoors warmth,
too deep to absorb; read.
Sort piles of jigsaw pieces,
logic wins. Write poem.
Home phone; mute TV; listen;
breathe.

The waiting game:
'He's in recovery – went well –
collect him in an hour.'
Whisky clouds spread across blue sky.
Sunshine, now.

2021 THE MATING GAME

[Insp by 'The Dating Game' Patsy Goodsir/QL 95, August 2021]
QL open comp (5th place) 2021-11/PUBLD

I dye my hair, but then again
it's mainly thick and will remain.
I always was a D (DD),
rest more than tea… if you could see!

I have a man whose separates lift:
he thinks my cups are quite a gift.
My matching bras and knickers do
what gentlemen (don't) repeat. True.

I've bought a pack of 6 or 8…
my sexy lips pout full estate.
I think that I can guarantee
much more to steam his glass of me.

No dating sight for me – I've found
one man's muscles (playful), abound.
My tummy turns him inside out,
the black de-robes (I think) his spout.

A nice new man won't do. The art:
releases (not his hair); each fart.
His warmth and humour glows so well,
that cheque book fattens quite pell-mell.

He's coming very fast; this bond:
a mating lark for life; so fond.
He tells the truth (just one tooth capped);
and one nose – you know – always tapped.

2021 PEARLY SKIES AT 30
Lothlorien Poetry Journal/2022-05 Blog

A perfect pearl within a pearly frame.
Is it too much to hope for many more?
A string to dance the Milky Way, its game
is far beyond mortality, before

first breath or last? I don't know what to write.
The scent of winter intrudes on dark sky.
I cannot flutter-wing, owl-angel flight
to shining seas, pearlescent, floating by.

I want to capture sweet meringues in snowfall;
to crystallise fresh mince pies/cake-drunk coating.
December disappoints as drizzly rainfall
and all the choirs of heaven's absence: floating.

Simply, fake champagne and Hyde Park Autumn,
russet-laughter, negligee, crook caught-em.

2021 THOSE PEARLS THAT WERE . . . TO SPRING
For the Many not the Few/Volume 24//2022-06/Amazon

Winter bleeds its berries until spring,
I cannot blanche brash hope, to pause so long
when daffodils might cheer my future mood.

I wait, feint hope, for tears bled into snow.
You know? White threads of fear bleed through slow veins.
Pearls are my eyes – I'm underwater now.

My daughter is the final – precious – pearl
to glow our greying skies, to memory loss,
decrepitude and ageing's outrageous scythe.

You understand? How can you? Don't ask now
how tomes of Shakespeare dance around his quills.
They're angel feathers... really? Dream again,

You nearly cannot fathom writs in water:
my maiden name (no, voyage) solicits nostalgia.
Supported by bare facts; and fragile flowers.

I've Wellbeing-ed into blisters of metatarsals;
self-help mounts like a library without card-index.
The pearls of thirty years itch imperfections.

Now, this freshwater necklace is beyond compare:
my Koh-i-noor of luminescent pain.
Diamond your mood (mine's simply pearlescent),

My gender-neutral daughter (now Trans/born male):
please may she have a future (hope, and smile).
My pearly whites' Anniversary... waiting snowdrops.

I hope you realise: I'm looking in the mirror, only now –today –
yesterday I was in a scallop shell, covering modesty with floaty golden
hair and – you know – hair comes in two shades (or, sometimes one).
As a child, I contemplated the head (black & white, did not realise
that true likeness on the wall of the children's home.
What a classic!
I'm Botticelli ever after, so, eat your heart in. Contemplate her nubile
form in youth. Let's not get bogged down with practicalities, (poets get
creative, above a certain age).
I was born (little better than Dickens' creations)and, after a brief spell,
my baldness raged into fire. I hope you're contemplating Venus rising:
emerging fully formed, everything in its right place.
Is your mirror misting now?
Consider the sleeping maiden (perfect in every way), not looking at you;
not interested; yet.   Next, contemplate that mirror (it's in your room
too);
Diego's young woman knows you are looking.
Will you rise to the occasion?
Will she turn and stare...
Breathe into your imagination, for now she's grown a little
(I don't mean, in the way of women – some do, some don't).
There's luggage at the back of the room; she's waiting
for what you might do. Has she married; does she care to look.
Susurrated by pain. Love? Worth? A husband?
No matter... combine the Art Gallery's wealth of images:
the female nude (nakedness banned on social media?);
not ogled in a boudoir/a harem/a cheap flat with paper-thin walls).
Think not of Giorgione/Gauguin/Boucher/Burne-Jones...
I am asking you to contemplate woman;
a real woman, at every age/and stage/and pound of flesh.
Mirror your own heavenly vision; the moment you want immortalised in
verse.
Have you risen to the occasion? Does it matter...
just; never forget: I am Venus, and
Thomas Crapper/Mr D'Arcy/or Hugh Grant are in the wings waiting
Bridget.
You're there now, aren't you? In the mirror; steaming.
And SHE (a woman), glances in the looking glass...
                    Have you found that rabbit hole (or potion); yet!

2022 POLYAMOROUS FLIGHT OF BOBOLINKS

['Whoso sees this little flower / by faith may clear behold...' Emily Dickinson]
Crystal 2022-07 on file

She sees this little flower, grown doubly-gold
after 100 years lived (fluting silver buds and windfalls).
The scent of florabundant grief, her crown-wreathed smile:
loved-lawn and lost, as oceans.

Her husband died too soon by fast-spreading dementia,
spring chicken over 90, feathers plucked.
My friend, 'going for gold', passed at the theatre's
milling concourse hall; his beloved wife
beside him; an audience of dandelion clocks.

Vibrant with life
(children fresh-faced out of Uni
spicy carnation, he died of cancer;
their coronavirus of daisies trampled to dust,
before kinglier years of babysitting descendants.

No clear bee holding fancies of pure faith,
dancing on a pinhead of Tinkerbell's joy:
here where snowdrops crowned a full pearl necklace.
Graveyard of an innocent girl's discarded earring.
Buried dreams – 0 to 365 –
yet, what are days for? What's love?

Each red, red rose of sharpest thrones has bled
paper boats and Pooh-sticks seating Aphrodite.
The Kiss/The Birth of Venus holds less charm
than chocolate hearts, or tides of papyrus flowers.
You understand? No poet (him)… my words:

I love you (let me count), like

these bloody blooms.

2005 LOVE ON THE THRONE
Tips/2008-03

I tear apart quilt words to scent-fresh pine,
dull routine absence hollows out my time:
a homely cesspit of free-flowing slime.
I need your cistern's flush, where loving's fine.

Although you rise where morning fails to shine,
no limescale builds to silt love into crime.
Air freshener bouquets - signatures of grime –
where moist to moist and skin to skin's a sign:

One flesh, one heart, one red rose that you're mine,
angelic choirs of snores tone me to rhyme.
No loveseat thrones such warm and comfy clime
and you will always be my Valentine.

I simply need your loving mess each day,
romancing me in passion's caring way.

2022 ON THE BRINK
WEB Star Issue 4/2022-04

It's time to say Goodbye to our old world,
the one we loved/ignored/or treated like Mother.
The buds of Spring – even now – are being unfurled;
yet we cannot remember our friend, or brother.

What's left is now? Just war, and that last trump?
We cannot even undaze our wine-fuelled play.
The just (in their safe havens, or have the hump),
for what we thought was ours in that last day.

Ukraine is on the brink; the Queen has Covid;
we've trashed Celebs and superstars to earth.
What we hear now of Peace/Wild Weather's horrid.
What hope may come, and visions of rebirth?

The world is more forgiving than a lover.
Is this wild hellebore brave for another…?

2022 THE BLUES AND YELLOWS OF MOTHER'S DAY
LANDSCAPES 2022-06//Amazon

Smashed the glass of Mother's Day:
no flimsy frame nor mirror.
Expendable/long-dead/unnamed
glass trashed to ornamental hell.
No shattered curve (feminine nor fine)
from family times of long ago.
Dreamed it all, that fairytale,
the young with happy smiles and flowers,
Wobbling in with tray piled high:
coffee cold/burnt toast/a mug
of juice/and marmalade sticky-sublime.
Finally, a card/a giggle/hug/then off to play.
Dream on, arthritic joints, just hope for coffee,
or kick him out to duties (clocks wound round),
a special Mother's Day (the young sleep late).
So late…my firstborn, waiting for a dove (crows
and wood pigeons, magpies) – strut your stuff
for heavenly featherdown and sparkling stars.
A blond child, laughing, would be doubly good.
Sleep on, my stillborn; none of this world's gain.
Remember? How your Grandma died too soon…
Grimm fairy tales (not pink nor sweet) today.
My love, my life, redeemed with tray, but later.
A simple feast; and Mamma Mia on Play.
Uncork the gin – glass to ease dull pain –
or just see dancing daffodils; and write.

2022 FATHER'S DAY 2022-1993
Wildfire Words 2022-07 Open/Website

It was the best day of the year,
that day you became a father
and I was hot, exhausted, tucked in bed,
while you made busy with phone calls – news –
before mobile phones/digital/live streaming.
Thank the gods no delivery recorded.

So proud, how you carried our second
       in your arms; cradled to the grave.
Tiny; early; late; far too late.

Proudly discombobulated – in the lift –
anaesthesia wearing thin:
you held my hand, proud husband/
father/man; that good news reigned,
running between SCBU and post-delivery ward.

You haven't stopped since: keeping us both happy.
What a delivery (9 weeks premature),
unlike that bouncing firstborn (2 weeks late).
Sterling silver; gold; platinum;
       multiplied.

Prouder than hell (if you would listen):
this tip of the iceberg - Pluto's –
where other men are simply lettuce.

No father – ever – did more; did better; survived
Father's Day Breakfast at a Vintage Inn.
Nothing at all compares... You deserve an OBE
(not much competition),
as the best father;
         ever.

2011 ANNIVERSARY (20 years)

PUBLD Crystal/Mar 2012

These flowers show you mean the world to me,
delivered, over breakfast, with surprise.
They show that love aims high, is blooming free
as one tall vase with rosebuds in his eyes.

The chocolates show that love grows fast, to share
its sweetness with the earth, through taste, consumes,
yet still is there another day. Lovely, bare
as newlyweds, when tiffs fade, touch resumes;

so bloom and fade and fall, then prickle, rise,
soft-folding to the scents of England's best.
It may not be the greatest. How time flies,
in hope that arms fold peacefully, at rest

with everything or nothing, hands tease, dare
to trace love lightly, light years, everywhere.
Two trace love, lightly, light years, everywhere,
with everything or nothing, hands tease, dare:

in hope that arms fold peacefully. At rest,
it may not be the greatest. How time flies,
soft-folding to the scents of England's best.
So bloom and fade and fall, then prickle, rise,

as newlyweds, when tiffs fade, touch resumes,
yet still is there another day. Lovely, bare.
Its sweetness (with the earth) through taste, consumes;
the chocolates show that love grows fast, two share,

as one tall vase with rosebuds in his eyes.
They show that love aims high, is blooming free,
delivered, over breakfast, with surprise.
These flowers show you mean the world to me.

Publisher.

inherit_theearth@btinternet.com

Notes

Printed by Amazon Italia Logistica S.r.l.
Torrazza Piemonte (TO), Italy

43459631R00058